THE GREAT LITTLE BOOK OF RICE DISHES

bowled over

Emma Summer

southwater

This edition is published by Southwater

Southwater is an imprint of Anness Publishing Ltd
Hermes House, 88–89 Blackfriars Road, London SE1
8HA; tel. 020 7401 2077; fax 020 7633 9499
www.southwaterbooks.com; info@anness.com

Published in the USA by Southwater, Anness Publishing
Inc., 27 West 20th Street, New York, NY 10011;
fax 212 807 6813

This edition distributed in the UK by The Manning
Partnership Ltd; tel. 01225 478 444; fax 01225 478 440;
sales@manning-partnership.co.uk

This edition distributed in the USA by National Book
Network; tel. 301 459 3366; fax 301 459 1705;
www.nbnbooks.com

This edition distributed in Canada by General Publishing;
tel. 416 445 3333; fax 416 445 5991; www.genpub.com

This edition distributed in Australia by Pan Macmillan
Australia; tel. 1300 135 113; fax 1300 135 103;
email customer.service@macmillan.com.au

This edition distributed in New Zealand by The Five Mile
Press (NZ) Ltd; tel. (09) 444 4144; fax (09) 444 4518;
fivemilenz@clear.net.nz

Publisher Joanna Lorenz
Managing Editor Linda Fraser
Designers Patrick McLeavey & Partners
Illustrator Anna Koska
Photographers Karl Adamson, Edward Allwright,
Steve Baxter, James Duncan, Michelle Garrett,
Amanda Heywood & Thomas Odulate
Recipes Carla Capalbo, Kit Chan, Jacqueline Clarke,
Joanna Farrow, Rafi Fernandez, Shehzad Husain,
Christine Ingram, Soheila Kimberley, Ruby Le Bois,
Liz Trigg, Laura Washburn & Steven Wheeler

Previously published as *The Little Rice Cookbook*
10 9 8 7 6 5 4 3 2 1

NOTES
For all recipes, quantities are given in both metric and
imperial measures and, where appropriate, measures are
also given in standard cups and spoons. Follow one set, but
not a mixture, because they are not interchangeable.
Standard spoon and cup measures are level.
1 tsp = 5ml, 1 tbsp = 15ml, 1 cup = 250ml/8fl oz
Australian standard tablespoons are 20ml. Australian read-
ers should use 3 tsp in place of 1 tbsp for measuring small
quantities of gelatine, cornflour, salt, etc.
Medium eggs are used unless otherwise stated.

THE GREAT LITTLE BOOK OF RICE DISHES

bowled over

Contents

Introduction

Rice is one of the world's oldest and most versatile foods. An excellent source of complex carbohydrates, it is high in fibre, provides useful quantities of B Group vitamins, and contains very little fat. The energy from rice is released slowly into the blood-stream, so it is not a quick-fix carbohy-drate like sugar. Considering that it cooks quickly and easily, with little or no advance preparation, can be used for an astonishing range of sweet and savoury foods, and is easily digested, it isn't hard to see why this grain continues to grow in popularity.

Rice grains come from a number of related aquatic cereal grasses. Originally cultivated mainly in Asia, paddy fields (the name "paddy" refers to the plant which yields the rice) are now a feature of the landscape in Europe and America, too.

Two-thirds of the world's peoples enjoy rice in some form every day, and new varieties are constantly being cultivated.

Rice is generally categorized as being either long or short grain. Long grain types, such as Patna and basmati, tend to retain their shape and remain separate when cooked, whereas the stubbier short grain varieties cook down to a creamy consistency which makes them perfect for puddings or risottos. The grains of certain short grain types tend to stick together when cooked, an attribute which makes them much sought after for sushi, rice cakes or croquettes. Some varieties, such as Thai rice, have characteristics of both types.

It is worth getting to know at least some of the different varieties of rice available.

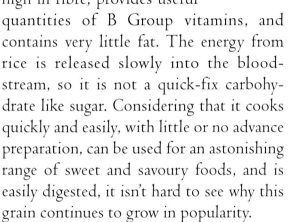

If you've never enjoyed the aroma of basmati, or been tempted by the texture of perfectly cooked arborio, you've missed some of the world's greatest culinary treats. New varieties and blends are constantly coming on to our supermarket shelves, giving us every opportunity to expand our repertoire of recipes. Two recent arrivals are the red rices from California and the Camargue.

We've travelled the world to bring you this collection. Dishes range from rissoles to risottos, and amply illustrate the scope of this simple ingredient. Whether you sneak a few stuffed vine leaves as a snack, or sit down with the family to a hearty chicken and prawn jambalaya, rice always adds interest to the menu.

Like pasta, rice combines perfectly with poultry, fish, shellfish (especially prawns) and vegetables. In these rice recipes, vegetarians are amply – and imaginatively – provided for, with dishes like Parsnip, Aubergine & Cashew Biryani sharing the limelight with Broccoli Risotto Torte. It is worth remembering, too, that rice contains no gluten, so a dessert like Thai Rice Cake is perfect for anyone on a gluten-free diet.

Other sweet suggestions include a delightful Moroccan pudding, scented with orange flower water and spiced with cinnamon, and a simple sundae served with raspberries, nuts and chocolate sauce.

If you've only ever viewed rice as a rather dreary accompaniment to a chilli or curry, now's the time to take a fresh look at a storecupboard standby that could well become one of your favourite foods.

7

Types of Rice

LONG GRAIN WHITE RICE

Perhaps the most familiar type of rice in the West, this is used mainly for savoury dishes. The rice is milled to remove the outer husk of the grain, then polished to remove the bran and give the white grains a sheen.

EASY-COOK RICE

Rice sold as "easy-cook" or "par-boiled" has been treated with high pressure steam before being milled. The steam hardens the outside of the grain, so cooking takes a little longer, but the grains stay separate and are fluffy. Purists claim there is a loss of flavour because of the treatment process.

BASMATI RICE

The name of this rice means "fragrance" in Hindi, and aptly describes this delicately flavoured long grain variety. Basmati rice benefits from being thoroughly rinsed, then soaked for about 10 minutes in cold water, before use. It cooks more quickly than regular long grain rice.

BROWN RICE

This is not a specific type of rice, but a term used to distinguish any grain which retains its bran coating. Also described as wholegrain rice, brown rice has a nutty flavour. Brown rice takes longer to cook than white; some cooks prefer to fry the grains for a minute or two before adding boiling water.

RISOTTO RICE

A collective name for several varieties of short grain rice, all of which cook to a creamy consistency while retaining a bit of "bite". Arborio is the best known type of risotto rice. The secret of a good risotto is lots of patience. The hot liquid must be added gradually, with each ladleful being absorbed before the next is stirred in. The only exception to this rule is paella. Here the stock is added to the rice all at once, and the dish is allowed to simmer without being stirred.

THAI RICES

Thai jasmine and Thai fragrant rice are delicately scented long grain varieties that have a characteristic stickiness when cooked. They cook very quickly and are best cooked with just one-and-a-quarter times the amount of water to rice. Salt is not usually added.

GLUTINOUS RICE

Also called "sticky rice", this term generally refers to a Chinese short grain rice which sticks together on cooking. The name, however, is misleading as the rice does not contain gluten. It is easy to pick up with chopsticks and can be easily shaped and rolled. Glutinous rice can be white or black and is often used for puddings, served with sugar and coconut cream.

SUSHI RICE

As the name suggests, this sticky Japanese short grain rice is used for making sushi, the popular raw fish and rice parcels.

RED RICE

Rice grown in the wild is a light red colour. New varieties which are being bred to recreate this fabulous colouring are now creating considerable interest. For red rice with a buckwheat flavour, try the semi-wild cultivar from the Camargue.

WILD RICE

Not a true rice, but an unrelated aquatic grass from Canada and North America. The long, dark brown grains are costly and take a long time to cook, but the resultant nutty flavour is highly prized. A form of smaller grain, cultivated "wild rice" is cheaper and more easily available. It is often sold blended with long grain rice.

Techniques

RINSING AND SOAKING

Basmati rice and wild rice both benefit from being rinsed in several changes of cold water, then soaked for about 10 minutes before being drained and cooked. The traditional way of rinsing the rice is to add it to a large bowl of water and swirl it gently with your fingers. Glutinous rice is also rinsed and then given a long soak.

COOKING IN AN OPEN PAN

Similar to the method for cooking pasta, this involves adding the rice to a large saucepan of lightly salted boiling water. When the mixture comes back to the boil, stir it once, then leave the rice to cook for 12–15 minutes (10 minutes for basmati or Thai rices). The grains will remain separate. After cooking, drain well, rinsing the rice in boiling water if you like. Leave to stand for 5 minutes before forking up.

COOKING BY ABSORPTION

Rinse the rice if necessary and put it in a saucepan. Add cold water to cover (amounts vary, so check package instructions, but as a general rule 225g/8oz/1 generous cup of long grain rice would require 600ml/1 pint/2½ cups) and add a little salt. Bring to the boil, stir once, then cover tightly and lower the heat so that the rice barely simmers. Cook basmati or Thai rice for 15 minutes; other long grain types for 20 minutes and easy-cook rice for slightly longer. Brown rice will need slightly more water and should be cooked for 25–35 minutes. After cooking, set the pan aside, still covered, for 5 minutes, then fluff up the grains and serve.

QUICK-START BROWN RICE

One way of cooking brown rice is to stir-fry the grains in a little butter before cooking them

in lightly salted boiling water. Use 15g/ ½oz/1 tbsp butter and 600ml/1 pint/2½ cups water for every 225g/8oz/1 cup of brown rice. Having added the water, bring it back to the boil. Stir and cover, then simmer for 35 minutes without lifting the lid. Fork up the grains and serve.

REHEATING

Cooked rice can be kept in the fridge in a sealed container for 2–3 days. To reheat, place the rice in a colander, rinse with boiling water, then set the colander over a saucepan of boiling water. Cover the pan with a cloth and steam for about 15 minutes. To reheat in the microwave, place the rice in a serving dish, cover loosely and heat on High (100% power). Four servings require 2–3 minutes cooking time and the rice should be forked up halfway through.

FAST FLAVOURINGS & QUICK TIPS

• Toss cooked rice with chopped fresh herbs just before serving.

• Fry sliced mushrooms in butter over a high heat until they are tender and most of the liquid has evaporated. Toss into the rice.

• Cook brown rice by the quick-start method, adding a little curry powder when stir-frying the grains. Toss the cooked rice with toasted cashew nuts or almonds or plumped sultanas.

• Make a simple confetti salad by dicing carrots and peppers of various colours very finely and tossing them with freshly cooked and cooled rice. Add a simple vinaigrette.

• Use vegetable stock instead of water for cooking rice by the absorption method.

• Cook rice by the open pan method. Drain but do not rinse with boiling water. Pack the rice in well greased dariole moulds, leave in a warm place for 3–4 minutes, then invert on individual plates. Holding the plate and the mould together, tap firmly on the work surface to release the rice. Lift off the moulds.

• Add bruised green cardamom pods and a cinnamon stick to rice pudding for an oriental flavour. Stir in rosewater just before serving.

11

Starters &
Snacks

Sushi

INGREDIENTS

TUNA SUSHI
3 sheets nori (paper-thin seaweed)
150g / 5oz very fresh tuna fillet, cut into thin strips
5ml / 1 tsp wasabi (horseradish mustard), thinned with water
6 young carrots, blanched
450g / 1lb / 4 cups cooked sushi rice
SALMON SUSHI
4 eggs, lightly beaten
2.5ml / ½ tsp salt
10ml / 2 tsp caster sugar
5 sheets nori
450g / 1lb / 4 cups cooked sushi rice
150g / 5oz very fresh salmon fillet, cut into thin strips
5ml / 1 tsp wasabi, thinned with water
½ small cucumber, cut into 5 batons

SERVES 10–12

1 Make the tuna sushi. Spread half a sheet of nori on a bamboo mat, lay strips of tuna lengthways across and season with the thinned wasabi. Place a blanched carrot next to the tuna and roll tightly. Seal the roll with water.

2 Place a square of non-stick baking paper on the bamboo mat and spread it with sushi rice. Centre the nori roll on top and wrap. Press to set, then cut into rounds. Make more tuna sushi in the same way.

3 Make the salmon sushi. Use the eggs, salt and sugar to make five simple flat omelettes in a non-stick frying pan.

4 Place a sheet of nori on a bamboo mat, cover with an omelette and trim to size. Spread a layer of rice over the omelette, then lay strips of salmon across the width. Spread the salmon lightly with wasabi, then place a cucumber baton next to the salmon. Roll up firmly, then press the roll so that it forms an oval. Cut into slices. Make more salmon sushi in the same way.

Red Rice Rissoles

INGREDIENTS

25g/1oz/2 tbsp butter
30ml/2 tbsp olive oil
1 large red onion, chopped
1 red pepper, seeded and chopped
2 garlic cloves, crushed
1 fresh red chilli, finely chopped
225g/8oz/generous 1 cup risotto rice
1 litre/1¾ pints/4 cups vegetable stock
4 drained sun-dried tomatoes in oil, chopped
30ml/2 tbsp tomato purée
10ml/2 tsp chopped fresh oregano
45ml/3 tbsp chopped fresh parsley
*150g/5oz/1¼ cups Red Leicester cheese, cut
into 12 pieces*
1 egg, beaten
115g/4oz/1 cup dried breadcrumbs
oil, for deep frying
salt and ground black pepper

SERVES 6

1 Melt the butter in the oil in a large saucepan and fry the onion, pepper, garlic and chilli for 5 minutes. Add the rice and stir-fry for 2 minutes more.

2 Pour in the vegetable stock and add the sun-dried tomatoes, tomato purée and chopped oregano. Season with salt and pepper to taste. Bring to the boil, stirring occasionally, then lower the heat, cover and allow to simmer for 20 minutes.

3 Tip the mixture into a bowl and stir in the chopped parsley. Allow to cool, then chill until firm. When cold, shape the mixture into 12 even-size balls, using your hands. Press a nugget of Red Leicester cheese into the centre of each rice ball.

4 Roll the rice balls in the beaten egg and then coat them in the breadcrumbs. Place the rissoles on a plate and chill again in the fridge for about 30 minutes. Deep fry the rissoles in batches in hot oil for 3–4 minutes, reheating the oil as necessary. Drain the rissoles on kitchen paper and keep hot. Serve with a side salad, if liked.

14

Stuffed Tomatoes & Peppers

INGREDIENTS

2 ripe beefsteak tomatoes
1 green pepper
1 yellow or orange pepper
60ml/4 tbsp olive oil, plus extra for drizzling
2 onions, chopped
2 garlic cloves, crushed
50g/2oz/½ cup blanched almonds, chopped
75g/3oz/scant ½ cup long grain rice, boiled and drained
30ml/2 tbsp chopped fresh mint
30ml/2 tbsp chopped fresh parsley
45ml/3 tbsp sultanas
150ml/¼ pint/⅔ cup boiling water
45ml/3 tbsp ground almonds
salt and ground black pepper
chopped mixed herbs, to garnish

SERVES 4

1 Preheat the oven to 190°C/375°F/ Gas 5. Cut the tomatoes in half and scoop out the pulp and seeds with a teaspoon. Drain the shells upside-down on kitchen paper. Chop the tomato flesh roughly.

2 Cut the peppers in half through the stems. Scoop out the seeds. Arrange the peppers, hollows-up, on a baking sheet. Brush with 15ml/1 tbsp of the oil and bake

for 15 minutes. Transfer to a shallow ovenproof dish, add the tomato shells and season with salt and ground black pepper.

3 Heat the remaining oil in a frying pan and fry the onions for 5 minutes until golden. Stir in the garlic and chopped almonds and fry over a medium heat for 1 minute more.

4 Remove the pan from the heat and stir in the rice, chopped tomatoes, mint, parsley and sultanas. Season with salt and pepper and divide the mixture among the tomato and pepper shells.

5 Pour the boiling water around the stuffed vegetables. Bake, uncovered, for 20 minutes, then scatter the ground almonds over the top of the tomatoes and peppers. Drizzle with a little extra olive oil. Bake for 20 minutes more, or until the shells are tender and the rice filling is turning golden. Garnish with the chopped mixed fresh herbs and serve immediately.

Rice & Mozzarella Croquettes

INGREDIENTS

*115g/4oz/generous ½ cup long grain rice,
freshly boiled
2 eggs, lightly beaten
75g/3oz/½ cup mozzarella cheese, grated
115g/4oz/1 cup dried breadcrumbs
oil, for deep-frying
salt and ground black pepper
fresh dill sprigs, to garnish*

AÏOLI
*1 egg yolk
few drops of lemon juice
1 large garlic clove, crushed
250ml/8fl oz/1 cup olive oil*

MAKES ABOUT 16

1 Drain the cooked rice thoroughly. Cool slightly, then tip into a bowl and stir in the eggs and grated mozzarella, with salt and pepper to taste.

2 Shape the mixture into 16 equal-size balls. Spread out the breadcrumbs in a shallow dish, add the rice balls and shake the dish to coat them thoroughly. Press the crumbs on well and chill the croquettes for 20 minutes.

3 Meanwhile, make the aïoli. Put the egg yolk, lemon juice and garlic into a small, deep bowl. Add salt and pepper to taste. Gradually whisk in the oil, a drop at a time at first, then in a steady stream, until the mixture is thick and glossy. Cover and chill.

4 Deep-fry the rice croquettes in batches in hot oil for 4–5 minutes or until crisp, reheating the oil as necessary. Drain on kitchen paper and keep hot. As soon as all the rice croquettes are cooked, garnish them with dill and serve with the aïoli.

Risotto-stuffed Aubergines

INGREDIENTS

4 small aubergines
105ml / 7 tbsp olive oil
1 small onion, chopped
175g / 6oz / scant 1 cup risotto rice
750ml / 1¼ pints / 3 cups vegetable stock
15ml / 1 tbsp white wine vinegar
fresh basil sprigs, to garnish
TOPPING
25g / 1oz / ⅓ cup grated Parmesan cheese
15ml / 1 tbsp pine nuts
SPICY TOMATO SAUCE
300ml / ½ pint / 1¼ cups passata
(puréed tomatoes)
5ml / 1 tsp curry paste
pinch of salt

SERVES 4

1 Preheat the oven to 200°C/400°F/Gas 6. Cut the aubergines in half lengthways. Using a sharp knife, cut the flesh criss-cross fashion into neat cubes, then cut round the shells and ease the cubes out. Brush the shells with 30ml/2 tbsp of the oil and place on a baking sheet. Bake for 15 minutes.

2 Heat the rest of the oil in a saucepan. Fry the aubergine cubes with the onion for 3–4 minutes until softened. Stir in the rice and stock and simmer for 15 minutes. Add the vinegar.

3 Raise the oven temperature to 230°C/450°F/ Gas 8. Spoon the rice mixture into the aubergine shells. Sprinkle the Parmesan and pine nuts on top. Bake for 5 minutes to brown the topping.

4 Meanwhile, make the sauce by heating the passata with the curry paste and salt in a small saucepan. Spoon the sauce on to four large plates, position two stuffed aubergine halves on each and garnish with basil sprigs. Serve at once.

Stuffed Vine Leaves with Garlic Yogurt

INGREDIENTS

225g/8oz packet preserved vine leaves
1 onion, finely chopped
4 spring onions, finely chopped
60ml/4 tbsp chopped fresh parsley
10 large mint sprigs, chopped
finely grated rind of 1 lemon
2.5ml/½ tsp crushed dried red chillies
7.5ml/1½ tsp fennel seeds, crushed
175g/6oz/scant 1 cup long grain rice
120ml/4fl oz/½ cup olive oil
300ml/½ pint/1¼ cups boiling water
150ml/¼ pint/⅔ cup thick natural yogurt
2 garlic cloves, crushed
salt
lemon wedges and mint leaves, to garnish
(optional)

SERVES 6

1 Rinse the vine leaves in plenty of cold water. Put into a bowl, cover with boiling water and soak for 10 minutes. Drain well, then dry on kitchen paper.

2 Mix the onion, spring onions, parsley, mint, lemon rind, chillies, fennel seeds and rice in a bowl. Stir in 25ml/1½ tbsp of the olive oil. Season with salt and mix well.

3 Flatten a vine leaf, veins uppermost, on a flat surface. Cut off any stalk. Place a heaped teaspoon of the rice mixture near the stalk end, fold the stalk end over, fold in the sides, then roll up to make a cigar shape. Repeat to make about 28 stuffed leaves.

4 Place any remaining leaves in the bottom of a large heavy-based pan. Arrange the stuffed vine leaves on top in a single layer. Spoon over the remaining oil, then pour in the boiling water.

5 Invert a small plate over the stuffed vine leaves to keep them submerged in the water. Cover the pan and cook over a very low heat for 45 minutes.

6 Meanwhile mix the yogurt and garlic together in a small bowl. Transfer the stuffed leaves to a serving plate. Garnish with lemon wedges and mint, if you like. Serve warm or cold, with the garlic yogurt.

Meat &
Poultry Dishes

Rice, Beef & Broad Bean Koftas

INGREDIENTS

115g/4oz/generous ½ cup long grain rice
450g/1lb lean minced beef
115g/4oz/1 cup plain flour
3 eggs, beaten
115g/4oz/1 cup podded broad beans, thawed
if frozen, skinned
30ml/2 tbsp chopped fresh dill
25g/1oz/2 tbsp butter
1 large onion, chopped
2.5ml/½ tsp ground turmeric
1.2 litres/2 pints/5 cups water
salt and ground black pepper
chopped fresh parsley, to garnish
naan bread, to serve

SERVES 4

3 Melt the butter in a large saucepan and fry the onion for 3–4 minutes until golden. Stir in the turmeric, cook for 30 seconds, then add the water. Bring to the boil.

1 Bring a saucepan of lightly salted water to the boil. Add the rice and par-cook for 4 minutes, then drain thoroughly. Tip into a bowl and add the minced beef, flour and eggs, with salt and pepper to taste. Knead until well blended.

2 Add the skinned broad beans and dill. Knead again until the mixture is firm and pasty. Shape into eight large balls, place on a plate and chill for 15 minutes.

4 Add the meatballs to the pan. Lower the heat and simmer for 45–60 minutes, until the meatballs are fully cooked and the sauce has reduced to about 250ml/  8fl oz/1 cup. Tip the mixture into a serving dish, garnish with the parsley and serve with naan.

Turkish Lamb Pilau

INGREDIENTS

40g / 1½oz / 3 tbsp butter
1 large onion, finely chopped
450g / 1lb lamb fillet, trimmed and cut into
small cubes
2.5ml / ½ tsp ground cinnamon
30ml / 2 tbsp tomato purée
45ml / 3 tbsp chopped fresh parsley
115g / 4oz / ½ cup ready-to-eat dried apricots,
halved
75g / 3oz / ¾ cup pistachio nuts, chopped
450g / 1lb / 2¼ cups long grain rice, rinsed
salt and ground black pepper
flat leaf parsley, to garnish

SERVES 4

1 Heat the butter in a large heavy-based pan. Add the onion and cook until soft and golden. Move the onion to the side of the pan and add the lamb  cubes. Brown on all sides, then sprinkle with the cinnamon and season with pepper. Stir, cover and cook gently for 10 minutes.

2 Add the tomato purée to the pan, then add enough water to cover the meat. Stir in the chopped fresh parsley. Bring to the boil, lower the heat, cover the pan and allow to simmer gently for 1½ hours or until the meat is tender.

3 Add enough water to the pan to make the liquid up to about 600ml / 1 pint / 2½ cups. Stir in the apricots, pistachios and rice. Bring to the boil, lower the heat, cover tightly and simmer for 20 minutes, or until the rice is cooked and the liquid has been absorbed. Taste the pilau and adjust the seasoning.

4 Spoon the pilau into a warmed serving dish and garnish with the flat leaf parsley. Serve at once.

COOK'S TIP

It is important that the meat retains its tenderness. Check the lamb from time to time while it is cooking, and add more water if necessary.

24

Thai Fried Rice with Pork

INGREDIENTS

45ml/3 tbsp corn oil
1 onion, chopped
2–3 garlic cloves, chopped
115g/4oz tender boneless pork, cubed
2 eggs, beaten
450g/1lb/4 cups cooked rice
30ml/2 tbsp fish sauce
15ml/1 tbsp dark soy sauce
2.5ml/½ tsp caster sugar
GARNISH
4 spring onions, finely sliced
2 fresh red chillies, sliced
1 lime, cut into wedges
1 small omelette, cut into strips

SERVES 4

1 Heat the oil in a wok or large frying pan. Stir-fry the onion with the garlic until softened, then add the pork and stir-fry until it is fully cooked.

2 Pour in the beaten eggs, stirring them into the pork mixture with a wooden spatula. Continue to stir over the heat until the eggs are scrambled.

3 Add the rice and stir gently to coat. Toss the mixture over the heat, taking care to prevent the rice from sticking to the pan.

4 Add the sauces and sugar. Mix well. When the rice is hot, tip the mixture into warmed individual serving bowls. Garnish with the spring onions,  chillies and lime wedges and arrange the strips of omelette on top. Serve at once.

French Beans, Rice & Beef

INGREDIENTS

25g/1oz/2 tbsp butter
1 large onion, chopped
450g/1lb braising steak, cubed
2 garlic cloves, crushed
5ml/1 tsp each ground cinnamon, cumin and turmeric
450g/1lb tomatoes, chopped
30ml/2 tbsp tomato purée
350ml/12fl oz/1½ cups water
350g/12oz French beans, trimmed and halved
salt and ground black pepper
RICE
275g/10oz/1½ cups basmati rice, soaked
140g/1½oz/3 tbsp butter
2–3 saffron strands, soaked in 15ml/1 tbsp boiling water

SERVES 4

1 Melt the butter in a large heavy-based pan and fry the onion until golden. Move it aside and brown the beef cubes, then stir in the garlic, spices, tomatoes, tomato purée and water. Season with salt and pepper. Bring to the boil, lower the heat and simmer for 30 minutes, then add the beans and cook for 15 minutes more, until the meat is tender and most of the liquid has evaporated.

2 Cook the drained rice in lightly salted boiling water for 5 minutes. Lower the heat and simmer for 10 minutes, then drain, rinse under hot water and drain again.

3 Melt 15g/½oz/1 tbsp of the butter in the clean pan. Stir in a third of the rice. Spread about half the meat mixture on top. Continue to layer the mixtures until all are used, ending with rice. Melt the remaining butter and drizzle it over. Cover tightly and steam for 30–45 minutes over a low heat.

4 Spoon 45ml/3 tbsp of the rice into a bowl and stir in the strained saffron liquid. Pile the remaining rice and beef mixture into a warmed serving dish, sprinkle the saffron rice on top and serve.

Yogurt Chicken & Rice

INGREDIENTS

40g / 1½oz / 3 tbsp butter
1.5kg / 3–3½lb chicken
1 large onion, chopped
250ml / 8fl oz / 1 cup chicken stock
2 eggs
475ml / 16fl oz / 2 cups natural yogurt
2–3 saffron strands, soaked in 15ml / 1 tbsp
boiling water
5ml / 1 tsp ground cinnamon
450g / 1lb / 2¼ cups basmati rice, soaked
75g / 3oz / ½ cup zereshk or redcurrants
salt and ground black pepper
herb salad, to serve

SERVES 6

1 Melt 25g/1oz/2 tbsp of the butter in a large flameproof casserole. Add the chicken, with the chopped onion. Cook, turning the chicken frequently, until it is browned on all sides and the onion has softened.

2 Add the stock, with seasoning if needed. Bring to the boil, lower the heat and simmer for 45 minutes or until the chicken is cooked and the stock has reduced by half.

3 Drain the chicken, reserving the stock, and remove the skin and bones. Cut the flesh into large pieces and place in a large bowl.

4 Beat the eggs with the yogurt, strained saffron water and cinnamon. Add salt and pepper to taste. Pour over the chicken, stir to coat, then marinate for up to 2 hours.

5 Cook the drained rice in lightly salted boiling water for 5 minutes. Lower the heat and simmer for 10 minutes, then drain, rinse under hot water and drain again. Lift the chicken pieces out of the marinade and set them aside. Stir half the rice into the yogurt marinade.

6 Preheat the oven to 160°C/325°F/Gas 3. Grease a large ovenproof dish, about 10cm/4in deep. Spread the rice and yogurt mixture on the base, arrange the chicken pieces on top and then add the plain rice. Sprinkle with the berries.

7 Pour over the reserved chicken stock, dot with the remaining butter, cover tightly with foil and bake for 35–45 minutes.

8 Remove the dish from the oven and place on a cold, dampened dish towel for a few minutes. Run a knife around the inner rim, invert a platter on top of the dish and turn the rice "cake" out. Serve in wedges, with a herb salad.

Chicken & Prawn Jambalaya

INGREDIENTS

50g / 2oz / 4 tbsp lard
2 chickens, about 1.5kg / 3–3½lb each, jointed
450g / 1lb raw smoked gammon, rinded and diced
3 onions, finely sliced
50g / 2oz / ½ cup plain flour
2 x 400g / 14oz cans chopped tomatoes
2 green peppers, seeded and sliced
2–3 garlic cloves, crushed
10ml / 2 tsp chopped fresh thyme
500g / 1¼lb / 3 cups long grain rice
1.2 litres / 2 pints / 5 cups water
2–3 dashes of Tabasco sauce
24 raw Mediterranean prawns, peeled and deveined, tails left intact
6 spring onions, finely chopped
45ml / 3 tbsp chopped fresh parsley
salt and ground black pepper

SERVES 8–10

1 Melt the lard in a large heavy-based pan. Fry the chicken pieces, gammon and onions, turning occasionally, for 15–20 minutes, until the chicken is golden brown on all sides. Using a slotted spoon, transfer the mixture to a dish.

2 Lower the heat, sprinkle the flour into the fat remaining in the pan and cook, stirring constantly, until the mixture is pale golden. Stir in the chopped tomatoes, green peppers, garlic and thyme. Cook, stirring, until the mixture forms a thick sauce, then return the chicken mixture to the pan and cook for 10 minutes, stirring occasionally.

3 Stir in the rice, with salt and pepper to taste. Pour in the water, add the Tabasco and bring to the boil. Lower the heat, add the prawns and cook until the prawns are pink and the rice has absorbed the liquid. Both chicken and rice should be tender.

4 Stir in the spring onions with 30ml/2 tbsp of the chopped parsley. Spoon the jambalaya on to a heated serving platter, garnish with the remaining chopped parsley and serve at once.

30

Chicken Biryani

INGREDIENTS

30ml / 2 tbsp oil
1 onion, thinly sliced
2 garlic cloves, crushed
1 fresh green chilli, finely chopped
15ml / 1 tbsp finely chopped fresh root ginger
*675g / 1½lb chicken breasts, skinned, boned
and cubed*
45ml / 3 tbsp curry paste
1.5ml / ¼ tsp salt
1.5ml / ¼ tsp garam masala
3 tomatoes, cut into thin wedges
275g / 10oz / 1½ cups basmati rice, soaked
1.5ml / ¼ tsp ground turmeric
2 bay leaves
4 green cardamom pods
4 cloves
6 cashew nuts

SERVES 4

1 Preheat the oven to 190°C/375°F/Gas 5. Heat the oil in a large frying pan. Fry the onion for 5–7 minutes, until lightly browned. Add the garlic, chilli and ginger and fry for 2 minutes more. Add the chicken and fry for 5 minutes, stirring.

2 Stir in the curry paste, salt and garam masala. Cook for 5 minutes. Add the tomatoes and cook for 3–4 minutes more. Remove from the heat.

3 Bring a large saucepan of lightly salted water to the boil. Add the drained rice and the turmeric. Cook for 10 minutes or until the rice is almost tender. Drain, tip into a bowl and toss with the bay leaves, cardamoms, cloves and cashew nuts.

4 Layer the rice and chicken mixture in a shallow ovenproof dish, finishing with a layer of rice. Cover the dish with foil and bake in the oven for about 15 minutes, or until the chicken is tender. Serve hot.

Fish & Seafood Dishes

Rice & Prawn Layer

INGREDIENTS

2 large onions, sliced and deep-fried
300ml / ½ pint / 1¼ cups natural yogurt
30ml / 2 tbsp tomato purée
60ml / 4 tbsp green masala paste
30ml / 2 tbsp lemon juice
5ml / 1 tsp cumin seeds
5cm / 2in piece of cinnamon stick
4 green cardamom pods
450g / 1lb raw king prawns, peeled and deveined
225g / 8oz / 2 cups small button mushrooms
175g / 6oz / generous 1 cup thawed frozen peas
450g / 1lb / 2¼ cups basmati rice, soaked
300ml / ½ pint / 1¼ cups water
3–4 saffron strands, soaked in
90ml / 6 tbsp milk
25g / 1oz / 2 tbsp ghee (clarified butter)
salt

SERVES 4–6

1 Mix the onions, yogurt, tomato purée, masala, lemon juice, cumin seeds, cinnamon, cardamoms and a little salt in a bowl. Stir in the prawns, mushrooms and peas. Mix well, cover and set aside in a cool place for 2 hours.

2 Grease the bottom of a heavy-based frying pan and add the prawn mixture, with any juices. Drain the rice and spread it evenly on top.

3 Pour the water all over the surface of the rice. Using a spoon handle, make random holes through the rice. Strain the saffron milk and spoon a little into each hole. Dot with ghee.

4 Place a foil round directly on top of the rice. Cover tightly and cook over a low heat for 45–50 minutes. Toss the mixture gently and serve at once.

Smoked Fish Kedgeree

INGREDIENTS

450g / 1lb mixed smoked fish
300ml / ½ pint / 1¼ cups milk
175g / 6oz / scant 1 cup long grain rice
1 lemon slice
50g / 2oz / ¼ cup butter
1 onion, finely chopped
10ml / 2 tsp garam masala
2.5ml / ½ tsp grated nutmeg
15ml / 1 tbsp chopped fresh parsley
salt and ground black pepper
fresh flat leaf parsley and 2 hard-boiled
eggs, halved, to serve

SERVES 6

1 Poach the un-cooked smoked fish in the milk for 10 minutes, until it flakes when test-ed with the tip of a knife. Drain, dis-carding the milk, and flake the fish.

Place it in a bowl and add any smoked fish that does not require cooking.

2 Then bring a saucepan of lightly salted water to the boil. Add the rice and the lemon slice and cook for 12 minutes until the rice is just ten-der. Drain well.

3 Melt the butter in a large heavy-based saucepan. Add the chopped onion and cook until softened, then stir in the rice and fish. Shake the pan to mix the ingredients thoroughly. Toss over the heat for 2 minutes.

4 Stir in the garam masala, grated nutmeg and parsley, and add salt and pepper to taste. Tip the mixture into a warmed dish, garnish with the flat leaf parsley and the hard-boiled eggs and serve at once.

Lebanese Fish with Rice

INGREDIENTS

juice of 1 lemon
45ml / 3 tbsp corn oil
900g / 2lb cod steaks
4 large onions, chopped
5ml / 1 tsp ground cumin
2–3 saffron strands, soaked in 15ml / 1 tbsp
boiling water
1 litre / 1¾ pints / 4 cups fish stock
450g / 1lb / 2¼ cups long grain rice
50g / 2oz / ⅔ cup pine nuts, lightly toasted
salt and ground black pepper
chopped fresh parsley, to garnish

SERVES 4–6

1 Mix the lemon juice with 15ml/1 tbsp of the oil in a shallow dish. Add the fish steaks, turn to coat thoroughly, then cover and marinate for 30 minutes.

2 Heat the remaining oil in a large saucepan. Fry the onions for 5–6 minutes, stirring occasionally. Drain the fish, reserving the marinade, and add the steaks to the pan. Fry for 1–2 minutes on each side, then add the cumin and a little salt and pepper.

3 Strain over the saffron water, then add the fish stock and reserved marinade. Bring to the boil, lower the heat and simmer for 8–10 minutes, until the fish is almost cooked.

4 Using a slotted spoon, transfer the fish steaks to a platter. Add the rice to the stock. Bring to the boil, lower the heat and simmer for 15 minutes.

5 Arrange the fish steaks on top of the rice. Cover tightly and steam for 15–20 minutes over a low heat. Transfer the fish to a plate, then spoon the

rice on to a large flat platter. Arrange the fish on top, sprinkle with the pine nuts and garnish with the chopped fresh parsley. Serve at once.

Spanish Seafood Paella

INGREDIENTS

60ml/4 tbsp olive oil
225g/8oz monkfish, skinned and cubed
3 prepared baby squid, body cut into rings and
tentacles chopped
1 onion, chopped
3 garlic cloves, finely chopped
1 red pepper, seeded and sliced
4 tomatoes, peeled and chopped
225g/8oz/generous 1 cup risotto rice
450ml/¾ pint/1¾ cups fish stock
150ml/¼ pint/⅔ cup white wine
4–5 saffron strands, soaked in 30ml/2 tbsp
boiling water
75g/3oz/¾ cup frozen peas
115g/4oz cooked, peeled prawns
8 fresh mussels, scrubbed and debearded
salt and ground black pepper
chopped fresh parsley, to garnish
lemon wedges, to serve

SERVES 4

1 Heat 30ml/2 tbsp of the oil in a paella pan and stir-fry the monkfish cubes with the squid for 2 minutes. Tip into a bowl and set aside.

2 Heat the remaining oil in the clean pan and fry the onion, garlic and pepper until softened. Stir in the tomatoes and rice. Cook for 4 minutes, stirring, then add the fish stock, wine, strained saffron liquid and peas, with salt and pepper to taste.

3 Gently stir in the monkfish, squid and prawns. Push the mussels into the rice. Cover tightly. Cook gently for 30 minutes, until most of the stock has been absorbed and the mussels have opened. (Discard any that remain closed.)

4 Remove the paella from the heat. Leave to stand, covered, for 5 minutes. Sprinkle with the parsley and serve with lemon wedges.

Seafood Risotto

INGREDIENTS

60ml/4 tbsp sunflower oil
1 onion, chopped
2 garlic cloves, crushed
225g/8oz/generous 1 cup risotto rice
105ml/7 tbsp white wine
1.5 litres/2½ pints/6 cups hot fish stock
350g/12oz mixed seafood (raw prawns,
mussels, squid rings, clams)
grated rind of ½ lemon
30ml/2 tbsp tomato purée
15ml/1 tbsp chopped fresh parsley
salt and ground black pepper

SERVES 4

2 Add 150ml/¼ pint/⅔ cup of the hot stock. Cook, stirring constantly, until it has been absorbed. Stir in a similar amount of stock until it has been absorbed. Continue in this way until you have added about half the stock.

3 Stir in the mixed seafood and cook over a medium heat for about 2–3 minutes. Add the remaining half of the stock as before, until the rice is creamy and tender.

4 Stir in the lemon rind, tomato purée and the chopped fresh parsley. Season with plenty of salt and ground black pepper. The risotto should be served warm rather than piping hot.

1 Heat the oil in a large heavy-based saucepan and gently cook the onion and garlic for about 4–5 minutes until soft. Add the rice and stir into the  contents of the pan, to coat the grains with oil. Pour in the white wine and stir over a medium heat for 2–3 minutes until it has been absorbed.

COOK'S TIP
Heat the fish stock in a saucepan before you start preparing the risotto, and keep it on a low simmer. Adding it in small amounts while stirring is the secret of a smooth, creamy dish.

New Orleans Bacon & Seafood Rice

INGREDIENTS

30ml/2 tbsp corn oil
115g/4oz rindless smoked bacon rashers, diced
1 onion, chopped
2 celery sticks, chopped
2 large garlic cloves, chopped
5ml/1 tsp cayenne pepper
2 bay leaves
5ml/1 tsp dried oregano
2.5ml/½ tsp dried thyme
4 tomatoes, peeled and chopped
150ml/¼ pint/⅔ cup passata (puréed tomatoes)
350g/12oz/1¾ cups long grain rice
475ml/16fl oz/2 cups stock
175g/6oz skinned haddock fillets, cubed
115g/4oz cooked, peeled prawns
salt and ground black pepper
2 spring onions, chopped, to garnish

SERVES 4

1 Preheat the oven to 180°C/ 350°F/Gas 4. Heat the oil in a flameproof casserole and fry the bacon until crisp. Add the chopped onion and celery and stir until soft and golden brown.

2 Add the chopped garlic, cayenne, dried herbs and chopped tomatoes, with salt and pepper to taste. Stir in the passata, rice and stock. Bring to the boil.

3 Stir the fish cubes into the rice mixture. Cover tightly. Put the casserole in the oven and bake for 20–30 minutes, until the rice is just tender.

4 Stir in the prawns and heat through. Sprinkle with the chopped spring onions and serve at once.

COOK'S TIP

For a special-occasion garnish, add a whole cooked prawn, in the shell, and a spring onion tassel, to each portion.

Vegetarian Dishes & Accompaniments

Broccoli Risotto Torte

INGREDIENTS

225g/8oz broccoli, cut into tiny florets
50g/2oz/4 tbsp butter
30ml/2 tbsp olive oil, plus extra for greasing
1 onion, chopped
2 garlic cloves, crushed
1 large yellow pepper, seeded and sliced
225g/8oz/generous 1 cup risotto rice
120ml/4fl oz/1/2 cup dry white wine
1 litre/1¾ pints/4 cups vegetable stock
115g/4oz/1⅓ cups grated Parmesan cheese
4 eggs, separated
salt and ground black pepper
tomato slices and chopped parsley, to garnish

SERVES 4

43

1 Blanch the broccoli in boiling water for 3 minutes, drain and set aside. Melt the butter in the oil in a frying pan. Fry the onion, garlic and pepper until soft.

2 Stir in the rice, cook for 1 minute, then pour in the wine. Cook, stirring constantly, until it is absorbed. Pour in the stock and season well. Bring to the boil, lower the heat and simmer for 20 minutes, stirring occasionally.

3 Preheat the oven to 180°C/350°F/Gas 4. Lightly grease a deep 25cm/10in round cake tin and base line it with non-stick baking paper. Stir the cheese into the rice mixture, cool for 5 minutes, then beat in the egg yolks. Fold in the broccoli.

4 Whisk the egg whites to stiff peaks; fold them into the rice. Spoon into the prepared tin and bake for 1 hour, until risen, golden and still slightly wobbly in the centre. Cool slightly, then invert on a serving plate and peel off the paper and turn back on to a serving plate. Garnish with tomato slices and parsley. This torte is also good served cold.

Parsnip, Aubergine & Cashew Biryani

INGREDIENTS

1 small aubergine, sliced
3 onions
2 garlic cloves
2.5cm / 1in piece of fresh root ginger, roughly chopped
45ml / 3 tbsp water
60ml / 4 tbsp corn oil
175g / 6oz / 1½ cups unsalted cashew nuts
40g / 1½oz / ¼ cup sultanas
1 red pepper, seeded and sliced
3 parsnips, roughly chopped
5ml / 1 tsp ground cumin
5ml / 1 tsp ground coriander
2.5ml / ½ tsp chilli powder
120ml / 4fl oz / ½ cup natural yogurt
120ml / 4fl oz / ½ cup vegetable stock
275g / 10oz / 1⅓ cups basmati rice, soaked
25g / 1oz / 2 tbsp butter
salt and ground black pepper
fresh coriander sprigs and quartered hard-boiled
eggs, to garnish

SERVES 4–6

1 Sprinkle the aubergine slices with salt and leave to drain for 30 minutes. Rinse the slices, pat dry and cut into bite-size pieces. Chop 1 onion roughly and place it in a food processor with the garlic and ginger. Add the water and process to a paste.

2 Slice the remaining onions finely. Heat 45ml/ 3 tbsp of the oil in a pan and fry the onions until golden. Drain well and place in a bowl. Stir-fry the cashews in the oil for 2 minutes, then add the sultanas and fry until they swell. Using a slotted spoon, transfer to the onions in the bowl. Stir-fry the aubergine, pepper and parsnips for 5 minutes, then lift out with a slotted spoon and set aside.

3 Heat the remaining oil and cook the onion paste until golden. Stir in the spices and cook for 1 minute, then lower the heat and stir in the yogurt, stock and aubergine mixture. Bring to the boil, lower the heat and simmer for 30 minutes. Tip the mixture into a baking dish and set aside.

4 Cook the drained rice in salted boiling water for 5 minutes, until tender but undercooked. Drain and mound on top of the vegetable mixture. Push a long spoon handle through the mixture and scatter the reserved onion mixture evenly on top. Dot with butter and cover with foil and a tight-fitting lid.

5 Bake the biryani for 35–40 minutes, then spoon on to a heated serving dish. Garnish with the fresh coriander and hard-boiled eggs and serve.

Wild Rice with Grilled Vegetables

INGREDIENTS

75g / 3oz / scant ½ cup wild rice
150g / 5oz / ⅔ cup long grain rice
1 large aubergine, thickly sliced
1 each red, yellow and green peppers, seeded and sliced
2 red onions, sliced
225g / 8oz / 2 cups brown cap or shiitake mushrooms
2 small courgettes, cut in half lengthways
olive oil, for brushing
30ml / 2 tbsp chopped fresh thyme
DRESSING
90ml / 6 tbsp extra virgin olive oil
30ml / 2 tbsp balsamic vinegar
2 garlic cloves, crushed
salt and ground black pepper

SERVES 4

1 Put both types of rice in a pan of water and add salt. Bring to the boil, then lower the heat, cover and cook for 30–40 minutes or until the rice is tender.

2 Meanwhile, make the dressing and grill the vegetables. Mix the olive oil, vinegar and garlic in a screw-top jar. Add salt and pepper to taste, close the lid tightly and shake until thoroughly blended.

3 Arrange the aubergine, peppers, onions, mushrooms and courgettes on a grill rack. Brush with the olive oil and cook under a hot grill for 8–10 minutes until well browned. Turn the vegetables occasionally and brush with oil.

4 Drain the rice mixture and tip it into a bowl. Shake the dressing again, pour half of it over the rice and mix. Spoon into a large serving dish and arrange the grilled vegetables on top. Drizzle the remaining dressing over and garnish with the thyme.

COOK'S TIP
Grilled vegetables taste and look wonderful when cooked on the barbecue. Use a solid ridged grill if you have one, to save slices from falling on to the coals.

46

Persian Rice & Lentils

Ingredients

450g/1lb/2¼ cups basmati rice, soaked
150ml/¼ pint/⅔ cup oil
2 onions, 1 chopped and 1 thinly sliced
2 garlic cloves, crushed
150g/5oz/⅔ cup green lentils, soaked and drained
600ml/1 pint/2½ cups vegetable stock
50g/2oz/⅓ cup raisins
10ml/2 tsp ground coriander
45ml/3 tbsp tomato purée
1 egg yolk, beaten
10ml/2 tsp natural yogurt
75g/3oz/6 tbsp ghee, melted
few saffron strands soaked in 10ml/2 tsp boiling water
salt and ground black pepper
fresh herbs, to garnish

Serves 8

1 Cook the drained rice in lightly salted boiling water for 3 minutes only. Drain well.

2 Heat 30ml/2 tbsp of the oil in a deep saucepan and fry the chopped onion and garlic for 5 minutes. Stir in the lentils, stock, raisins, coriander, tomato purée, and salt and pepper to taste. Bring to the boil, lower the heat, cover and simmer for 20 minutes.

3 Meanwhile, spoon 115g/4oz/1 cup of the cooked rice into a bowl and stir in the egg yolk and yogurt. Add plenty of salt and pepper. Mix well.

4 Heat two-thirds of the remaining oil in a pan. Spread the yogurt-flavoured rice over the base. Layer the plain rice and the lentil mixture in the pan, ending with the plain rice.

5 With a spoon handle, make three holes down to the bottom of the pan. Drizzle over the ghee. Bring to a high heat, then wrap the pan lid in a clean, wet dish towel and fit on top. When steam appears, lower the heat and simmer for 30 minutes. Fry the sliced onion until browned. Drain well.

6 Keeping the lid on, stand the pan of rice in cold water to loosen the golden crust on the bottom. Scoop about 60ml/4 tbsp of the plain rice into a bowl, strain over the saffron water and mix lightly.

7 Toss the rice and lentil mixture and mound it on a platter. Scatter the saffron rice on top. Break up the rice crust on the bottom of the pan and place it around the mound. Scatter the fried onion over, garnish with fresh herbs and serve.

Risotto alla Milanese

INGREDIENTS

25g / 1oz / 2 tbsp butter
1 large onion, finely chopped
275g / 10oz / 1½ cups risotto rice
150ml / ¼ pint / ⅔ cup dry white wine
5ml / 1 tsp saffron strands soaked in
15ml / 1 tbsp boiling water
1 litre / 1¾ pints / 4 cups vegetable stock
salt and ground black pepper
Parmesan cheese shavings, to garnish
GREMOLATA
2 garlic cloves, crushed
60ml / 4 tbsp chopped fresh parsley
finely grated rind of 1 lemon

SERVES 4

3 Add 600ml/ 1 pint/2½ cups of the stock to the saucepan. Simmer, stirring frequently, until it has been absorbed. Gradually add the remaining stock, a ladleful at a time, until the rice is tender and creamy. Allow each quantity of stock to be absorbed before adding the next (it may not be necessary to add it all).

4 Season the risotto with plenty of salt and pepper. Transfer it to a serving dish. Scatter lavishly with the Parmesan shavings and gremolata. Serve hot.

1 Make the gremolata by mixing the garlic and parsley in a bowl. Stir in the grated lemon rind and set aside.

2 Melt the butter in a heavy-based saucepan. Add the onion and fry over a low heat for 5 minutes. Stir in the rice until well coated. Cook for 2 minutes, until it is translucent, then add the wine and strain in the saffron liquid. Cook for 3–4 minutes, until the liquid has been absorbed.

Nutty Rice & Mushroom Stir-fry

INGREDIENTS

45ml / 3 tbsp sunflower oil
450g / 1lb / 4 cups cooked long grain rice
1 small onion, roughly chopped
225g / 8oz / 2 cups field mushrooms, sliced
50g / 2oz / ½ cup hazelnuts, roughly chopped
50g / 2oz / ½ cup pecan nuts, roughly chopped
50g / 2oz / ½ cup blanched almonds, roughly chopped
60ml / 4 tbsp chopped fresh parsley
salt and ground black pepper

SERVES 4–6

1 Heat half the oil in a wok. Add the rice and stir-fry for 2–3 minutes over a moderately high heat. Remove the rice from the wok and set aside. Then heat the remaining oil in the wok and stir-fry the chopped onion for 2 minutes, until softened.

2 Stir the sliced mushrooms into the wok with the onion. Toss over the heat for 2 minutes more.

3 Add all the nuts to the wok and stir-fry for 1 minute. Return the rice to the wok and stir-fry for 3 minutes. Add plenty of salt and pepper to taste. Stir in the chopped fresh parsley and serve at once.

COOK'S TIP

This is a wonderful way of using up leftover rice. Try brown rice, as a variation, and add cashews instead of almonds.

Festive Rice

INGREDIENTS

450g / 1lb / 2¼ cups Thai fragrant rice
60ml / 4 tbsp oil
2 garlic cloves, crushed
2 onions, finely sliced
5cm / 2in piece of fresh turmeric, peeled and
crushed
750ml / 1¼ pints / 3 cups water
350ml / 12fl oz / 1½ cups coconut milk
1–2 lemon grass stems, bruised
ACCOMPANIMENTS
omelette strips
2 fresh chillies, shredded
cucumber chunks
tomato wedges
deep-fried onions
prawn crackers

SERVES 8

1 Wash the rice in several changes of water. Drain well. Heat the oil in a wok and gently fry the garlic, onions and turmeric for 3–4 minutes, until the onions have softened, but not browned.

2 Stir in the rice until coated, then pour in the water and coconut milk. Add the lemon grass. Bring to the boil, lower the heat and simmer for 15 minutes, until all the liquid has been absorbed.

3 Remove the pan from the heat, cover with a clean dish towel and a tight-fitting lid and leave to stand in a warm place for 15 minutes.

4 Lift out the lemon grass and discard. Spread the rice mixture on a platter and garnish with the accompaniments. Serve at once.

52

Tomato Rice

INGREDIENTS

30ml / 2 tbsp corn oil
2.5ml / ½ tsp onion seeds
1 onion, sliced
2 tomatoes, sliced
1 orange or yellow pepper, seeded, roughly chopped and cut into chunks
5ml / 1 tsp grated fresh root ginger
1 garlic clove, crushed
5ml / 1 tsp chilli powder
30ml / 2 tbsp chopped fresh coriander
1 potato, diced
7.5ml / 1½ tsp salt
50g / 2oz / scant ½ cup frozen peas
400g / 14oz / 2 cups basmati rice, soaked
750ml / 1¼ pints / 3 cups water

SERVES 4

1 Heat the oil in a large saucepan and fry the onion seeds for about 30 seconds. Add the sliced onion and fry for 5 minutes more until they are lightly toasted.

2 Add the sliced tomatoes, pepper, ginger, garlic, chilli powder, fresh coriander, diced potato, salt and peas. Stir-fry over a medium heat for 5 minutes more.

3 Stir in the drained rice until well coated. Pour the water over and bring to the boil, then lower the heat slightly, cover tightly and cook for 12–15 minutes. Remove the rice from the heat, leaving the lid in place, and set aside for 5 minutes. Tip into a warmed serving dish, fork up the rice and serve.

53

Puddings & Desserts

Caramel Rice Pudding

INGREDIENTS

50g / 2oz / 5 tbsp short grain pudding rice
75ml / 5 tbsp demerara sugar
400g / 14oz can evaporated milk, made up to
600ml / 1 pint / 2½ cups with water
knob of butter
2 crisp eating apples
1 small fresh pineapple
10ml / 2 tsp lemon juice

SERVES 4

1 Preheat the oven to 150°C/300°F/Gas 2. Lightly grease a soufflé dish. Put the rice in a sieve and wash thoroughly under cold water. Drain well and tip into the soufflé dish.

2 Add 30ml/2 tbsp of the demerara sugar to the dish. Pour on the diluted evaporated milk and stir. Dot the surface with butter. Bake for 2 hours, then leave to cool for 30 minutes.

3 Meanwhile, core and slice the apples. Peel and core the pineapple and cut it into chunks. Put the fruit in a bowl. Add the lemon juice and toss lightly. Preheat the grill to the maximum heat.

4 Sprinkle the remaining sugar over the baked pudding. Grill until the sugar has caramelized. Leave to stand for 5 minutes, to allow the caramel topping to harden, then serve with the fresh fruit.

Moroccan Rice Pudding

INGREDIENTS

25g / 1oz / ¼ cup blanched almonds, chopped
450ml / ¾ pint / 1¾ cups very hot water
150g / 5oz / ¾ cup short grain pudding
rice, rinsed
25g / 1oz / 2 tbsp butter
7.5cm / 3in piece of cinnamon stick
pinch of salt
2.5ml / ½ tsp almond essence
400g / 14oz can condensed milk, made
up to 600ml / 1 pint / 2½ cups with
semi-skimmed milk
30ml / 2 tbsp orange flower water
toasted flaked almonds and ground cinnamon,
to decorate

SERVES 6

1 Process the almonds in a blender or food processor until very fine, then add 120ml/4fl oz/ ½ cup of the hot water and process again. Strain through a sieve into a large saucepan, pressing the nut pulp against the mesh with a spoon to extract as much liquid as possible.

2 Stir the remaining hot water into the almond "milk" and bring to the boil. Add the rice and half the butter to the pan, then add the cinnamon stick. Stir

in the salt and almond essence. Pour in half the diluted condensed milk mixture and stir well.

3 Bring to the boil, stirring constantly, then simmer over the lowest possible heat for 1–1½ hours, stirring in the remaining milk mixture towards the end of the cooking time, until the pudding is thick and creamy. Stir in the orange flower water.

4 Pour the rice pudding into a warmed serving bowl, sprinkle with the flaked almonds and dot with the remaining butter. Dust the ground cinnamon over the top and serve.

COOK'S TIP
This is delicious with a topping of Greek-style yogurt and a drizzle of clear honey. Use a delicately scented honey, such as orange blossom.

Souffléed Rice Pudding

INGREDIENTS

*65g / 2½oz / 5 tbsp short grain pudding
rice, rinsed
45ml / 3 tbsp clear honey
750ml / 1¼ pints / 3 cups milk
2.5ml / ½ tsp vanilla essence
2 egg whites
5ml / 1 tsp grated nutmeg*

SERVES 4

1 Place the rice, honey and milk in a heavy-based saucepan. Bring to just below boiling point, then simmer over the lowest possible heat for 1–1¼ hours,  stirring occasionally, until most of the liquid has been absorbed.

2 Preheat the oven to 220°C/425°F/Gas 7. Lightly grease a 1 litre/1¾ pint/4 cup ovenproof dish. Away from the heat, stir the vanilla essence into the rice mixture and set the saucepan aside to cool slightly.

3 Whisk the egg whites in a clean, dry bowl until soft peaks form. Using a large metal spoon, fold them lightly and evenly into the rice mixture. Tip the mixture into the prepared dish and level the surface.

4 Sprinkle with grated nutmeg and bake in the oven for 15–20 minutes, until the pudding is well risen and golden brown. Serve hot.

Fruited Rice Ring

INGREDIENTS

65g/2½oz/5 tbsp short grain pudding
rice, rinsed
900ml/1½ pints/3¾ cups milk
5cm/2in piece of cinnamon stick
175g/6oz/1 cup dried fruit salad
175ml/6fl oz/¾ cup orange juice
oil, for brushing
45ml/3 tbsp caster sugar
thinly grated rind of 1 small orange
whipped cream, to serve (optional)

SERVES 4

1 Place the rice, milk and cinnamon stick in a large saucepan. Bring to the boil, then simmer over the lowest possible heat for about 1½ hours, stirring occasion-

ally, until all the liquid has been absorbed.

2 Meanwhile, mix the dried fruit salad and orange juice in a second pan. Bring to the boil, lower the heat, cover and simmer for about 1 hour, until the fruit is tender and no liquid remains. Brush a 1.5 litre/2½ pint/6 cup ring mould lightly with oil.

3 Remove the cinnamon stick from the rice. Gently stir in the caster sugar and grated orange rind. Spread out the fruit on the base of the ring tin. Spoon the rice

over, smoothing it down firmly. Cover with clear film and chill for 3–4 hours.

4 Run a knife around the rim of the mould to loosen the rice ring. Invert a serving dish on top and carefully turn both mould and plate over. Serve with a spoonful of whipped cream, if liked.

Thai Rice Cake

INGREDIENTS

*225g / 8oz / generous 1 cup Thai fragrant rice
or jasmine rice
1 litre / 1¾ pints / 4 cups milk
115g / 4oz / ½ cup caster sugar
6 cardamom pods, cracked open
2 bay leaves
300ml / ½ pint / 1¼ cups whipping cream
6 eggs, separated*

TOPPING

*300ml / ½ pint / 1¼ cups double cream
200g / 7oz / scant 1 cup low-fat cream cheese,
softened
5ml / 1 tsp vanilla essence
grated rind of 1 lemon
40g / 1½oz / 3 tbsp caster sugar
soft berry fruits and sliced star fruit and kiwi
fruit, to decorate*

SERVES 8–10

1 Grease and base line a deep 25cm/10in round cake tin. Bring a large saucepan of unsalted water to the boil and cook the rice for 3 minutes. Drain the rice thoroughly.

2 Return the rice to the pan. Add the milk, sugar, cracked cardamoms and bay leaves. Bring to the boil, then lower the heat and simmer for 20 minutes, stirring occasionally. Tip the mixture into a bowl and set it aside to cool.

3 Remove the bay leaves and card-amom husks from the mixture. Beat in the whipping cream, then the egg yolks. Preheat the oven to 180°C/ 350°F/Gas 4.

4 Whisk the egg whites in a clean, dry bowl until soft peaks form. Fold into the rice mixture. Spoon into the prepared tin and bake for 45–50 minutes, until risen and golden brown. The centre should be slightly wobbly – it will firm up as it cools.

5 Chill the cooked rice cake overnight in the tin, then turn out on a large serving plate. Whip the double cream until stiff, then mix with the cream cheese, vanilla essence, lemon rind and sugar.

6 Cover the top and sides of the cake with the cream mixture, swirling it attractively. Decorate with the soft berry fruits and the sliced star fruit and kiwi fruit.

Rice Condé Sundae

INGREDIENTS

50g / 2oz / 4 tbsp short grain pudding rice
600ml / 1 pint / 2½ cups milk
5ml / 1 tsp vanilla essence
2.5ml / ½ tsp ground cinnamon
45ml / 3 tbsp sugar
To Serve
raspberries, strawberries or blueberries,
thawed if frozen
chocolate sauce and toasted flaked
almonds (optional)

SERVES 4

1 Put the rice, and milk, vanilla essence, cinnamon and sugar into a saucepan. Bring to the boil, stirring constantly, then lower the heat and simmer for 30–40

minutes, stirring occasionally and adding more milk if needed, until the grains are soft.

2 Spoon the mixture into a bowl and set aside to cool, stirring occasionally to prevent a skin from forming. When cold, chill the mixture in the fridge.

3 Just before serving, stir the mixture well. Spoon it into four sundae dishes. Top with raspberries, strawberries or blueberries and add the chocolate sauce and toasted flaked almonds, if using.

COOK'S TIP
Rice puddings are wonderfully versatile.
Try this with dates or apricots stewed in a syrup
flavoured with rosewater. For a very rich pudding,
use half milk and half cream; for slimmers, use
semi-skimmed milk and top with fresh fruit
and natural yogurt.

Mangoes with Sticky Rice

INGREDIENTS

*115g/4oz/generous ½ cup white glutinous
(sticky) rice
175ml/6fl oz/¾ cup thick coconut milk
45ml/3 tbsp sugar
pinch of salt
2 ripe mangoes
strips of pared lime rind, to decorate*

SERVES 4

1 Rinse the glutinous rice thoroughly in several changes of cold water. Leave to soak overnight in a bowl of fresh, cold water.

2 Drain the rice and spread it in an even layer in a steamer lined with muslin or cheese-cloth. Cover and steam for about 20 minutes, or until the grains are tender.

3 Meanwhile, skim off 45ml/3 tbsp from the top of the coconut milk and set it aside. Heat the remaining coconut milk with the sugar and salt in a saucepan. Stir until the sugar dissolves, then bring to the boil. Pour into a bowl and cool slightly.

4 Tip the rice into a bowl and pour over the sweet-ened coconut milk. Stir well, leave to stand for 10–15 minutes so that the rice absorbs some of the liquid, then spoon into a serving dish.

5 Peel the mangoes and slice the flesh thinly. Arrange the fruit on top of the rice pudding and drizzle over the reserved coconut milk. Decorate the pudding with strips of lime rind.

63

Index